GRINDLEY POTTERY

A Menagerie

Mike Schneider

77 Lower Valley Road, Atglen, PA 19310

Photograph on Title Page

Natural looking horses are one of Grindley's best kept secrets, probably because they are so different than most of the rest of the company's output, and because so few are marked. This double figure on base measures 5-1/4 x 7 inches. It is not marked. Estimated value: $55. *Carson collection.*

Printed in China

ISBN: 0-7643-0085-7

Book Design by Michael William Potts

Library of Congress Cataloging-in-Publication Data

Schneider, Mike.
  Grindley pottery: a menagerie/ Mike Schneider.
    p.   cm.
  Includes bibliographical references and index
  ISBN 0-7643-0085-7 (pbk.)
  1. Grindley Artware Manufacturing Company--Catalogs. 2. Pottery--20th century--Ohio--Sebring--Catalogs. 3. Pottery animals--Catalogs.   I. Title.
NK4210.G72A4 1996
738.3'09771'39--dc20   96-242
                                        CIP

Published by Schiffer Publishing, Ltd.
77 Lower Valley Road
Atglen, PA 19310
Phone: (610) 593-1777
Fax: (610) 593-2002

Please write for a free catalog.
This book may be purchased from the publisher.
Please include $2.95 for shipping.
Try your bookstore first.

We are interested in hearing from authors with book ideas on related subjects.

Contents

This unmarked Grindley deer is 4-1/4 inches high. Estimated value: $18. *Oravitz Collection.*

Dedication

To Richard and Susan Oravitz, special friends whose hospitality, along with their willingness to share their pottery and knowledge, makes writing a book like this a very enjoyable experience.

See Photograph on next page

This unmarked jumping lamb stands 5-1/2 inches high. The orange and blue on white decoration, while not common, does appear in other places in the book. Estimated value: $15. *Oravitz Collection.*

Acknowledgments

Many thanks to Susan and Richard Oravitz, and Betty and Floyd Carson. I am indebted to them not only for allowing me to photograph their collections, but also for recognizing Grindley as an artistically pleasing and collectible pottery.

Introduction

While the Grindley Artware Manufacturing Company is a long way from being a household phrase among figural pottery collectors, its products are recognized by many as items worthy of display and sale at mid-range to upscale antique shows. Grindley figures are often found sitting in neatly arranged booths next to pieces made by Owens, Rookwood, and numerous other well-known and highly respected art potteries. This is especially true of the Art Deco-Egyptian style cats and similarly designed dogs. And while I have seen prices on these pieces as high as $85 each, I have never found a dealer who knew what one was if it did not have a paper label.

Figurines such as this stylized cat, and also the yellow dog, are often seen displayed at antique shows by dealers who handle good art pottery. Height is 6-1/4 inches. The piece is not marked. Estimated value: $20. *Oravitz Collection.*

Which speaks quite highly of Grindley. People who routinely deal in Fulper, Van Briggle, and all the rest of what was great about America's former pottery industry, feel an unmarked Grindley figure is good enough to sit among the best of their offerings.

That is why I wrote this book--because Grindley was creatively designed, imaginatively decorated, and has won the respect of those who know good pottery. I hope you enjoy being introduced to this exciting new collectible.

A dog to match the cat. It is shorter, however, only 4-1/2 inches high. Although other examples are marked, this one is not. Estimated value: $20. *Carson Collection.*

Chapter 1
History

The little known Grindley Artware Manufacturing Company operated in Sebring, Ohio, the home of several better known potteries such as Royal Copley (Spaulding), Stanford, and China Craft. It was active from 1933 to 1952. The company was started by Arthur Grindley Sr. and his son Arthur Grindley Jr. (If the name Arthur Grindley Jr. sounds familiar, it is because he later served as president of the Shawnee Pottery Company for a short time.) Both were experienced potters. Grindley Sr. is said to have been at a point in his career where the dinnerware pottery at which he was employed bored and frustrated him. He envisioned what eventually became Grindley Artware Manufacturing as a means to express his creativity.

They began modestly, working in the basement of the father's house. As business flourished, the small cellar became quite cramped. At that point the operation was moved to an old barn behind the house, which, although much more spacious, proved to be little more than a stopgap measure on the Grindleys' road to success. The final move took the pottery across the alley, where the family bought some property and built a state-of-the-art plant that eventually employed as many as 175 people.

All this transpired prior to February, 1947 when a night time fire claimed the plant in its entirety, leaving nothing but a worthless pile of rubble. The structure was rebuilt, but due to financial hardship and heavy foreign competition, it never approached its former strength. Post-fire employment is said to have peaked at about 25, and the company closed permanently in 1952.

A 5-3/4 inch high zebra with typical Grindley decoration.
Like many other pieces in the book, it is unmarked. Estimated
value: $25. *Carson Collection.*

Chapter 2
Keys to Identification

Grindley made figurines, salt and peppers, planters, pitchers and various other pieces. Identifying them can be challenging in the beginning. Familiarization and experience will make it easier.

The surest means of identification is an in-mold mark, backstamp, or paper label. Several of these are shown. All but two include the word Grindley. Unfortunately, of the three methods of marking, the firm relied most heavily on paper labels, the vast majority of which have disappeared during the roughly half century since they were applied. On to familiarization and experience.

This is the most common of the several paper labels the company used. Due to its unique shape, this label can sometimes identify a piece even if it is missing. On several occasions I have confidently purchased unmarked Grindley figures by recognizing the outline of the label where it had once been glued.

One of the best ways to identify a piece of pottery is by its shape and size. For example, the green jumping lamb below is not marked in any way. But an identical one in cobalt on page 92 carries a Grindley paper label. That leaves little doubt about the green one.

This green jumping lamb is not marked, but its identity is confirmed by another that is. Height is 5-1/2 inches. Estimated value: $20. *Carson Collection.*

Glaze (color) is also a good identifier. While neither the turtle nor the fox shown is marked, a fox on page 81 is. That identifies the fox shown here, while the glaze color confirms the turtle. More subtle but just as telling is the gold line decorating of each figure.

While neither of these pieces is marked, each can easily be confirmed as Grindley. The fox is the simpler case; it is identical to one on page 81 that has a Grindley paper label. The turtle requires a little more detailed explanation. Note that its glaze matches that of the fox exactly. While different potteries may use the same commercially prepared glazes, that doesn't necessarily mean they look the same on the finished product. Variations in the method or thickness of application, firing temperature, even the air in the building, will result in slightly different color tones. For such a close match to exist, it seems nearly certain that the pieces had to be made by the same company. The turtle measures 1-1/2 x 3-1/2 inches. The fox is 3-1/4 inches high. Estimated value: turtle $15, fox $15. *Oravitz Collection.*

And speaking of decorating, check out the pair of tan, black and brown hounds. The one on the left sports a Grindley paper label. Grindley did many different dogs, and some other animals, in this same manner. The style of decoration is as good as a signature.

The hound on the left is 2-3/8 inches high and has a Grindley paper label. The one on the right, 2-1/4 inches high, is not marked. The slight difference in size is common. The tan, black and brown color combination is not. Grindley used it on dogs and other animals. Collect Grindley and eventually you will be able to spot it from a great distance. Estimated value: $10 each. *Oravitz collection.*

The "gold lock" design with which Grindley collectors are so familiar has been used on the blue-green Art Deco donkey. That unique design confirms Grindley as the maker as surely as a paper label would.

Note the gold designs similar to locks on this 4-3/4 inch high unmarked donkey. They identify a piece as Grindley as sure as an inkstamp or paper label. Estimated value: $30. *Oravitz Collection.*

On naturalistic horses the gray hooves are perhaps the best identifier. They are characteristic of every naturalistic horse shown in this book, and of every one I have personally seen that is not in the book.

Many Grindley horses exhibit similar colors, this particular brown for the main body, with darker legs fading to white, and black mane and tail. But the best bet is to look at the hooves for the telltale Grindley gray. I can't positively state that the company did not use any other treatment on hooves simply because it is impossible to prove a negative, but I can tell you that I have never seen or heard of them any other way. Height of this horse is 3-3/4 inches. It is unmarked. Estimated value: $30. *Carson Collection.*

Lastly, watch for limited amounts of red paint brushed on with precise strokes, as used on the ears, eyes, nose, and mouth of the yellow horse. Tails were often painted red, too.

Learn these identifying characteristics and you will be a step ahead of the other Grindley collectors and dealers with whom you are competing.

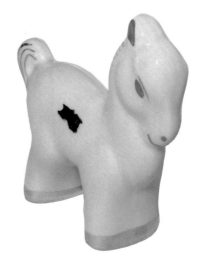

No doubt about this horse's maker; the Grindley paper label tells all. But even if it was absent, the red paint used for highlights on this style of figure gives one a pretty good indication that Grindley produced it. Height here is 4-3/4 inches. Estimated value: $18. *Oravitz Collection.*

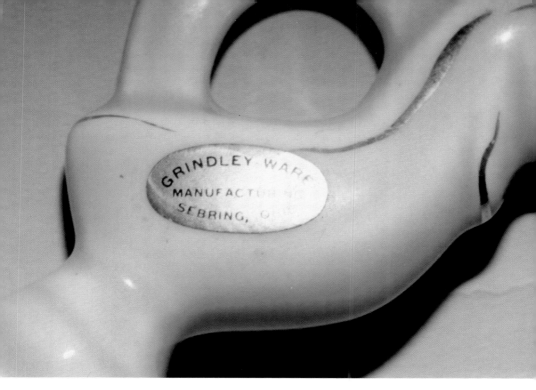

This paper label is from the chicken shaker on page 107.

The donkey on page 79 has this paper label while the one next to it has the more common black one.

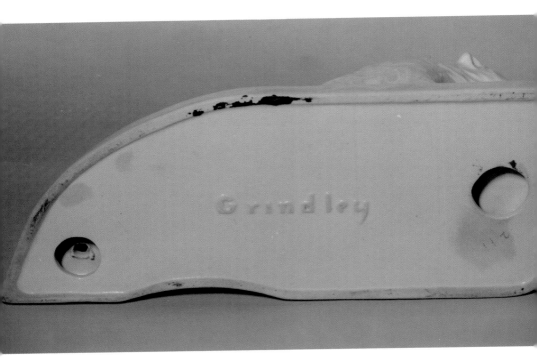

Mark of the white tiger on page 101. Many potteries made similar tigers, Grindley was one of the few that marked them.

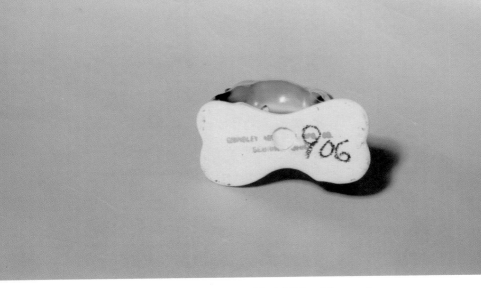

Gold inkstamp of the horse on page 19. A bit hard to see, it reads, "Grindley Art... Mfg Co. / Sebring Ohio," on two lines.

The first of two marks that do not include the word Grindley.

Grindley used this "Hand Painted" paper label a lot. I have also seen it on the works of other potteries, so it is not 100 percent foolproof. However, if you see it and the piece it is on is done in Grindley's style, as this yellow dog shaker is, it would seem safe to assume it is a Grindley piece until proven otherwise.

Chapter 3

Horses

Grindley made more figurines of horses than of any other subject of which I am aware. They can be divided into two specific groups, those that appear very lifelike in shape and coloring, and those that don't. The second group could be further divided into two subcategories, Art Deco, and fanciful.

Some collectors consider Grindley's lifelike horses to be the company's best work. Horse collectors in general seem to appreciate them, though not to the extent that they do Hagen-Renakers or Breyers.

The horse on the left stands 4 inches high, is unmarked. The one on the right, 3-1/8 inches high, has a gold stamp, "Grindley Artware Mfg. Co. / Sebring Ohio." This mark is shown on page 16. Estimated value: left $35, right $30. *Oravitz Collection.*

The 4-inch high horse on the left is a repeat of the one directly above, but with different markings. Note the paper label on its base. The double figure on the right is unmarked. Its height is 3-3/8 inches. Estimated value: left $30, right $45. *Carson Collection.*

An unmarked rearing horse, 7-1/2 inches high. Its bottom is shown. Estimated value: $95. *Carson Collection.*

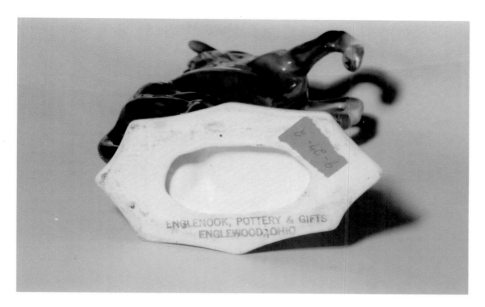

Although this says Englenook Pottery & Gifts, there is no doubt the horse was made by Grindley and what we see here is simply an inkstamp of a company that sold it.

Measurements of this figurine are 5-1/4 x 7-1/8 inches. It is not marked. This same piece in a darker color and photographed from the opposite side is shown on the title page. Note the addition of the gold line around the base of this one. Estimated value: $55. *Oravitz Collection.*

Borrowing from Henry Ford, it appears the Grindleys were happy to make a horse any color the customer wanted, as long as it was brown. Height of this one is 8-1/4 inches. It is not marked. Estimated value: $75. *Carson Collection.*

This big boy is 8-1/4 inches high without the base, 8-3/4 inches with it. Note the paper label. The bottom of this base is shown. Estimated value: $95. *Private Collection.*

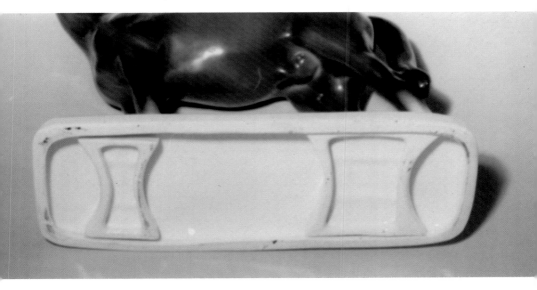

Bottom of the base of the above horse. Reinforcement pieces of the type shown here are not seen very often.

The grazing horse is 3-1/2 inches high.
Check its paper label, which is different
than any shown in Chapter 2: Keys to
Identification. The horse at the right is
3 inches high, unmarked. Estimated
value:top $30, bottom $25. *Carson
Collection.*

Another grazing horse, this one being 5-1/2 inches high. It is
unmarked. Estimated value: $60. *Carson Collection.*

This standing colt measures 6-5/8 x 5-1/2 inches. It is not marked. Estimated value: $60. *Carson Collection.*

A scratching horse, 5-1/4 x 7 inches. Look closely and you will see a Grindley paper label across the top of its hind quarters. Estimated value: $75. *Carson Collection.*

Each of these horses stands 4-1/2 inches high. The flower
decoration on the one with the paper label is rarely seen.
Estimated value: left $10, right $25. *Carson Collection.*

Same horse but with Grindley's classic gold "lock" decoration. Height of this one is 4-3/8 inches. The black paper label on back can barely be seen. Estimated value: $30. *Oravitz Collection.*

Height here is 4-1/8 inches. There is no mark. Estimated value: $18. *Oravitz Collection.*

This is the same as the white and gold horse but with a slight size difference, 4-1/2 inches high. Estimated value: $18. *Oravitz Collection.*

If this 8-1/2 inch high horse looks familiar, it is because it came from the same blank as the very natural looking one on page 22. That is a Grindley paper label on its back. Estimated value: $20. *Oravitz Collection.*

To me, this 4-1/4 x 5-1/2 inch horse is like one of those
specially made images that changes before your eyes. Most of
the time it appears very graceful and flowing and beautiful.
But once in awhile it strikes me as two people wearing a horse
costume with a front half and a back half, and they have yet
to learn to walk in step with each other. Estimated value: $30.
Carson Collection.

This one is one quarter inch longer than the green one, and unmarked. Estimated value: $20. *Oravitz Collection.*

A pink example. Estimated value: $20. *Private Collection.*

Here is a 7-1/4 inch high horse. It has a Grindley paper label
that does not show in the picture. Estimated value: $15.
Oravitz Collection.

A work horse, 7-1/2 inches high and unmarked. Estimated value: $20. *Oravitz Collection.*

Colt or fawn? For now, I guess, we will call it a colt. It is 5-3/4 inches high with a Grindley paper label. Estimated value: $30. *Carson Collection.*

Did you hear about the guy who crossed a dachshund with Dobbin? This must be the result. Measurements are 3-1/2 x 5-1/2 inches. It is not marked. Estimated value: $20. *Oravitz Collection.*

This pair is 5 inches high. Neither is marked. Estimated value: $15 each. *Oravitz Collection.*

A 4 inch high unmarked souvenir of Gettysburg, Pennsylvania. Estimated value: $10. *Oravitz Collection.*

This fellow measures 3 x 4-3/4 inches. That's a Grindley
paper label on its back. Estimated value: $10. *Oravitz Collec-
tion.*

Same measurements as above, different decoration. Also, no
paper label, and this one has an eye that is round instead of
triangular. Estimated value: $10. *Oravitz Collection.*

This horse is 3-1/8 inches high. It is not marked. Estimated value: $5. *Carson Collection.*

The height of this little colt is only 2-1/2 inches. It is unmarked. Estimated value: $5. *Oravitz Collection.*

Chapter 4
Dogs

Dogs are second only to horses in Grindley's output. In appearance they run from natural to fanciful. Some clearly display a strong Art Deco influence.

Grindley dogs without paper labels can often be found at very reasonable prices at antique shows and flea markets, probably because many dealers confuse them with cheap Japanese imitations that flooded the market following World War II.

More Grindley dogs are shown in Chapter 6: Salt and Pepper Shakers.

One of Grindley's most popular dogs among collectors, in teal and complete with gold locks, this guy stands 4-3/8 inches high. His unusual mark is, "Made in USA," incised. Estimated value: $35. *Oravitz Collection.*

A cobalt example, 4-1/2 inches high and unmarked. Estimated value: $35. *Oravitz Collection.*

This pink dog has less gold than the previous two examples.
Height is 4-1/2 inches. There is no mark. Estimated value:
$25. *Oravitz Collection.*

in your library. We would like to keep you informed about other publications from Schiffer Publishing Ltd.

TITLE OF BOOK: _____   ☐ hardcover
                                                ☐ paperback

☐ Bought at: _____
☐ Received as gift

COMMENTS: _____
_____
_____
_____

Name *(please print clearly)* _____

Address _____

City _____ State _____ Zip _____

☐ *Please send me a free Schiffer Arts, Antiques & Collectibles catalog.*

☐ *Please send me a free Schiffer Woodcarving, Woodworking & Crafts catalog*

☐ *Please send me a free Schiffer Military/Aviation History catalog*

☐ *Please send me a free Whitford Press Mind, Body & Spirit and Donning Pictorials &*
  Cookbooks catalog.

SCHIFFER BOOKS ARE CURRENTLY AVAILABLE FROM YOUR BOOKSELLER

SCHIFFER PUBLISHING LTD
77 LOWER VALLEY RD
ATGLEN PA 19310-9717

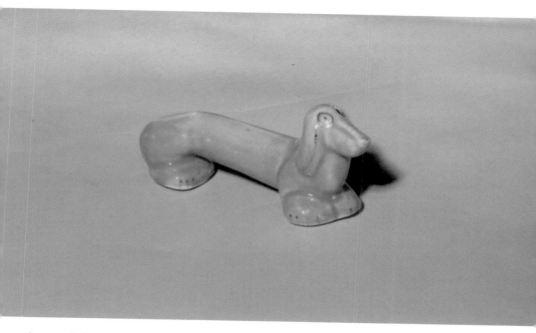

A second dog with a long pink nose. Stretched out it measures 2-1/2 x 5 inches. It is not marked. Estimated value: $15. *Carson Collection.*

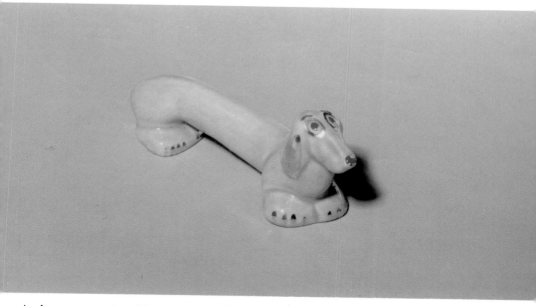

And a green version. Measurements of this one are 2-3/8 x 4-3/4 inches. Like the pink one, it is not marked. Estimated value: $15. *Oravitz Collection.*

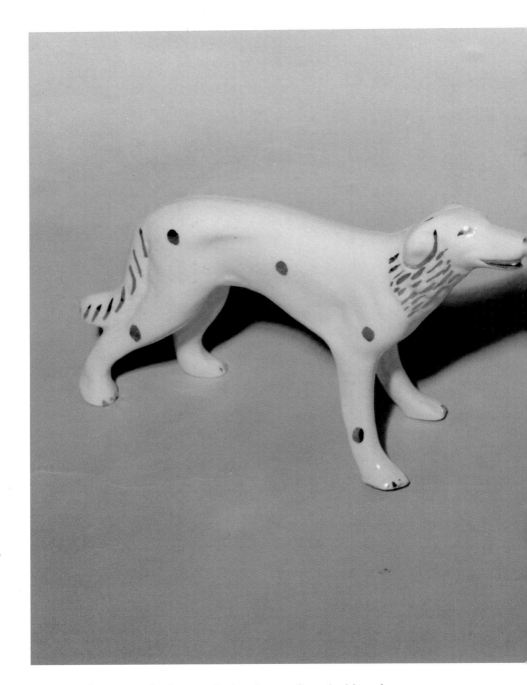

These borzois are both unmarked and unconfirmed, although
the gold trim and round dots certainly point strongly enough
to Grindley to include them here. Height on the left is 4-3/4
inches. Height on the right is 5-1/8 inches. Estimated value:
white with gold $15, blue $10. *Oravitz Collection.*

This unmarked dog measures 6 inches in length, 3 inches in height. Estimated value: $15. *Oravitz Collection.*

Here's a close cousin of the dog above. Unmarked, it is 2-1/4 inches high, 4-5/8 inches long. Estimated value: $10. *Oravitz Collection.*

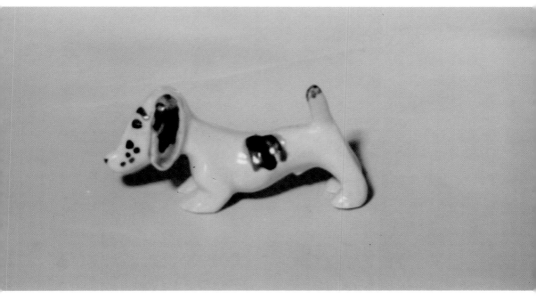

Same dog but with slightly different decoration, and photographed from a different angle. Also unmarked, it measures 2-1/2 x 4-3/8. Estimated value: $10. *Oravitz Collection.*

This dog stands 2-3/4 inches high. It is not marked. Estimated value: $10. *Private Collection.*

The unmarked dog on the left is 2-3/4 inches high, while the unmarked one on the right stands 3 inches. (In case you are wondering how we know all of these unmarked dogs are Grindley, flip back to page 12 to see one with a paper label.) Estimated value: $10. *Carson Collection.*

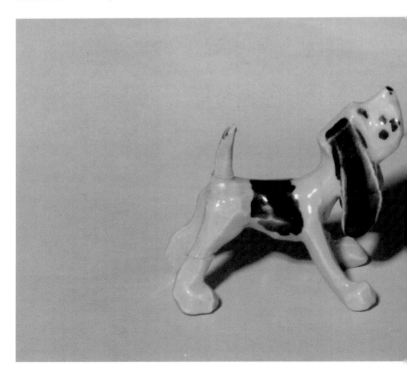

A St. Bernard, 4-1/2 x 5 inches. It has a partial paper label.
Estimated value: $15. *Private Collection.*

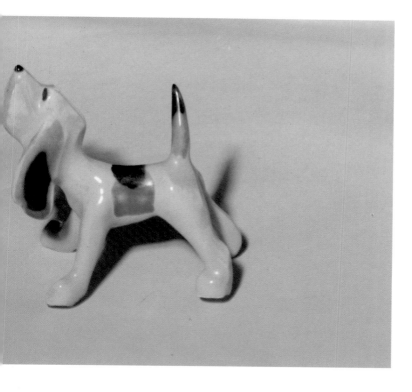

This dog measures 3-1/2 inches in height, is unmarked.
Estimated value: $10. *Oravitz Collection.*

This dog is the same as the one immediately above, but
painted differently, and possessing much greater mold detail.
Unmarked, it stands 3-3/4 inches high. Estimated value: $15.
Private Collection.

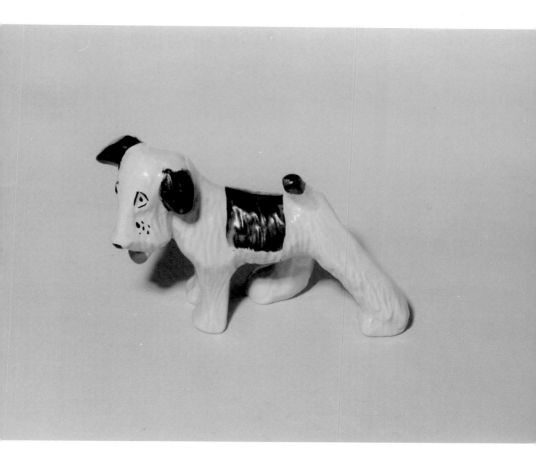

Same as the tan and brown version above but with different
decoration. Another difference is that this one has a paper
label. Height is 3-3/4 inches. Estimated value: $10. *Oravitz
Collection.*

A 3-1/2 inch high dog. It is not marked. Estimated value: $10. *Oravitz Collection.*

Left to right these guys stand 2-1/4, 1-3/4, and 1-7/8 inches
high. The one in the middle has a Grindley paper label, the
other two do not. Estimated value: $5 each. *Oravitz Collection.*

An English bulldog, 2-1/2 x 3-1/2 inches high, and un-marked. Estimated value: $10. *Oravitz Collection.*

Height here is 2 inches. Look closely and you will see the Grindley paper label across the dog's back. Estimated value: $5. *Oravitz Collection.*

This dog carries the "Hand painted / Made in U.S.A." paper label shown on page 17. The figure measures 1-3/8 x 2-1/2 inches. Estimated value: $5. *Oravitz Collection.*

This dog is similar to the mostly white model shown above but smaller, measuring only 2-7/8 inches in height as compared to 3-1/2 inches. Note the Grindley paper label on its back. Estimated value: $10. *Oravitz Collection.*

Here is both the small and large model, 3 and 3-5/8 inches
high. The shorter one has a paper label, the taller one is
unmarked. Estimated value: small $10, large $10. *Oravitz
Collection.*

This setter measures 2-7/8 x 4-1/2 inches. It carries both a
"Grindley" and a "hand painted" paper label. Estimated
value: $10. *Oravitz Collection.*

Chapter 5

Other Animals

Bears, donkeys, goats, and more. As you will see, the shapes of Grindley's other animals are usually quite realistic. You seldom find the colors that way, though. They are most often solid and bright pinks, blues, greens, etc., shades rarely seen in real animals. Hey, that's alright. After all, these things were made to decorate America's living rooms of the 1930s and 1940s, not the underbrush of its animal and game preserves.

One of Grindley's goodies that doesn't appear here, and that you will want to be on the lookout for, is a doe and fawn mounted on a base, similar to the double horses in Chapter 3.

An unmarked bear, 2-3/8 x 4-3/4 inches. Estimated value: $10. *Oravitz Collection.*

A pair of bears, also unmarked, and 4 inches high. Estimated
value: $15 each. *Oravitz Collection.*

This camel stands 5-3/4 inches high. It is unmarked. Estimated value: $15. *Oravitz Collection.*

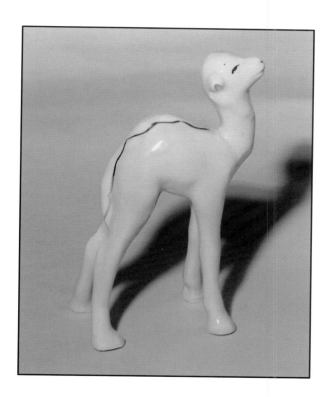

Another camel, also unmarked, and 5-3/8 inches high. Estimated value: $10. *Carson Collection.*

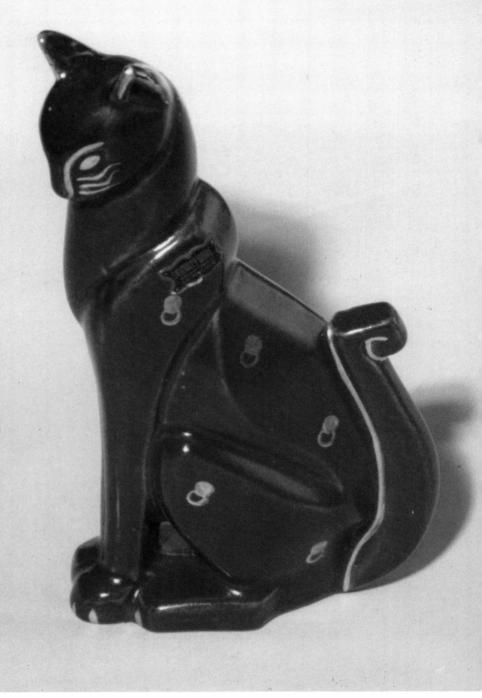

An Art Deco-Egyptian style cat, 6-3/4 inches high and sporting a Grindley paper label. Estimated value: $35. *Carson Collection.*

A pair of cats, these measuring 6-1/2 inches high. The one on
the left is not marked. Estimated value: left $20, right $25.
Carson Collection.

Height of this one is 6-1/8 inches. It is not marked. Estimated value: $20. *Oravitz Collection.*

This cow is not marked. It measures 2-7/8 x 4-1/2 inches.
Estimated value: $15. *Oravitz Collection.*

You may have heard of the small antlered animal called a key
deer that runs around southern Florida; now you have seen
its relative, the even smaller lock deer, just 6-5/8 inches high
and unmarked. Estimated value: $30. *Oravitz Collection.*

Same deer, no locks. Height is 6-1/2 inches. It is not marked.
Estimated value: $10. *Oravitz Collection.*

A pink one, also 6-1/2 inches high, also unmarked. Estimated value: $15. *Oravitz Collection.*

A yellow walking deer, as opposed to the three standing ones above. Its height, however, is the same, 6-1/2 inches. It is unmarked. Estimated value: $15. *Oravitz Collection.*

This deer stands 6 inches high. It is not marked. Estimated
value: $15. *Oravitz Collection.*

Probably a deer even though the body may look more like
that of a camel that has lost its hump. Height of this unmarked piece is 5-1/4 inches. Estimated value: $15. *Carson
Collection.*

A cobalt Deco donkey with the gold lock design. It is 5 inches high and unmarked. A teal model is shown on page 13. Estimated value: $30. *Private Collection.*

A 4-1/2 inch high donkey with a Grindley paper label.
Estimated value: $15. *Carson Collection.*

Same donkey, same paper label, same height as the white one.
But a little more significant if only for one small reason. As
you have no doubt figured out by now, about 90 percent of
the examples in this book belong to Richard and Susan
Oravitz. And this is the one that started them on their way, the
very first piece of Grindley in their collection. Estimated
value: $15. *Oravitz Collection.*

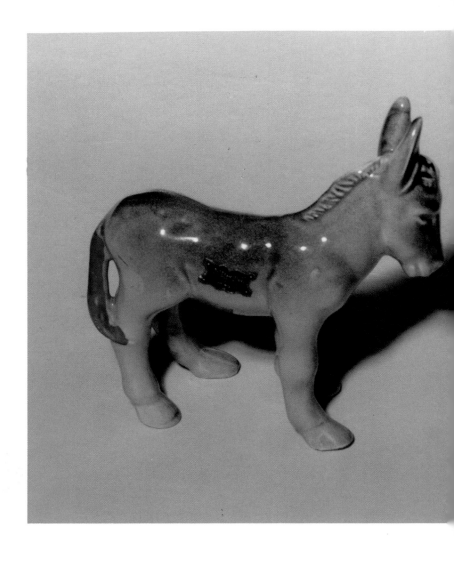

A pair of donkeys, each with a paper label, each with red trim. The one on the left stands 4-1/2 inches high, the one on the right 4 inches. Note that the red has begun to chip on the donkey on the right. This is common because, due to firing problems, nearly all potteries use red paint instead of red glaze. Should the red on any of your Grindley pieces chip, a little fingernail polish remover will take off the bad paint, while a steady hand and some Testors red gloss enamel will make the figure look as good as it did the day it left Sebring. Estimated value: left $10, right $10. *Oravitz Collection.*

Here is the final donkey, 3-1/4 inches high and unmarked. Estimated value: $10. *Oravitz Collection.*

This elephant is quite small, its height being but 2-1/4 inches.
It has a Grindley paper label. Estimated value: $10. *Oravitz*
Collection.

The foxes are 3-7/8 x 5 inches. The one in the middle, whose decoration is very similar to the standing bear on page 63, has a Grindley paper label. Estimated value: left $15, center $15, right $10. *Carson Collection.*

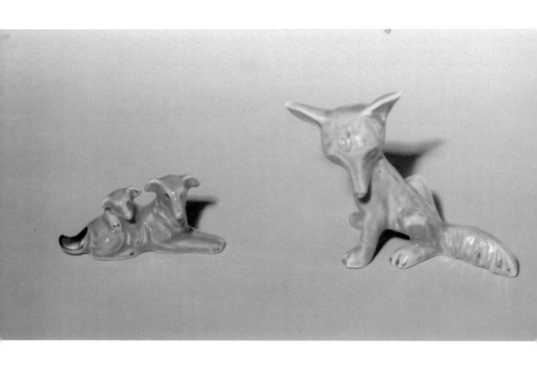

The dog and pup measure 1-3/4 x 3-1/4 inches. The fox is the
same as above but with a slightly thicker application of pink
glaze. Neither of these pieces is marked. Estimated value: dog
$15, fox $15. *Oravitz Collection.*

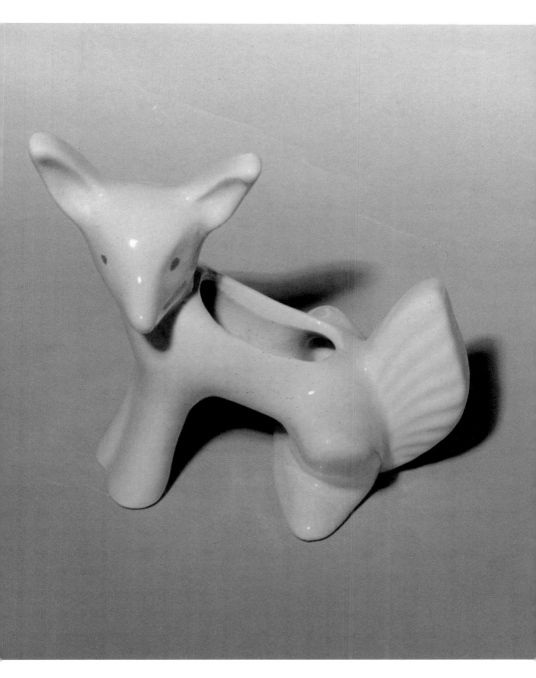

A 5 inch high unmarked fox planter. Although the characteristics of this piece appear to indicate Grindley origin, identification has not been confirmed and it may indeed have been made by another pottery. Estimated value: price not determined. *Oravitz Collection.*

The presence of the lock decoration leaves no doubt about the identity of this 5-1/2 inch high unmarked giraffe. Estimated value: $30. *Oravitz Collection.*

This giraffe stands 5-3/8 inches high. It is unmarked. Estimated value: $15. *Carson Collection.*

A 4-1/2 x 6 inch goat. The figure is unmarked. Estimated
value: $15. *Oravitz Collection.*

A rather tiny hippo, just 1-1/8 x 2 inches, and unmarked. This
piece has not been confirmed. Estimated value: $5. *Oravitz
Collection.*

This ox measures 2 x 4-1/4 inches. It is unmarked. Estimated value: $10. *Oravitz Collection.*

A white example, same size as the pink one. Estimated value:
$10. *Private Collection.*

And a yellow one. Note it has a broken horn. Estimated value:
$10 if perfect. *Private Collection.*

An unmarked ram, 4-5/8 inches high. Estimated value: $20.
Oravitz Collection.

Same piece as the pink ram but one-quarter inch taller at 4-7/8 inches. Like the pink example, it is unmarked. Estimated value: $20. *Oravitz Collection.*

This lamb is 2-3/8 inches high. It is not marked. Estimated value: $10. *Oravitz Collection.*

A jumping lamb, 5-3/4 inches high. It has a Grindley paper
label that cannot be seen in the picture. Estimated value: $30.
Carson Collection.

This one, 5-1/2 inches high, is unmarked. Its decal reads, "Lakeside on Lake Erie." If you were to look on page 149 of my previous volume, *California Potteries-The Complete Book,* you would find a similar piece made by Kay Finch. Estimated value: $30. *Oravitz Collection.*

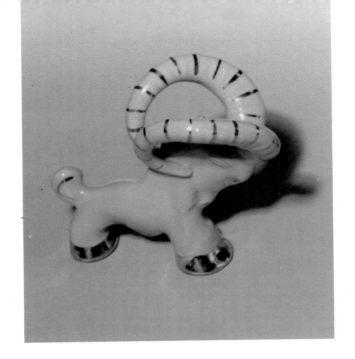

A pair of unmarked wild rams of some kind, getting ready to fight. Heights are 4 inches on the left, 4-3/8 inches on the right. Front views are shown. Estimated value: $15 each. *Oravitz Collection.*

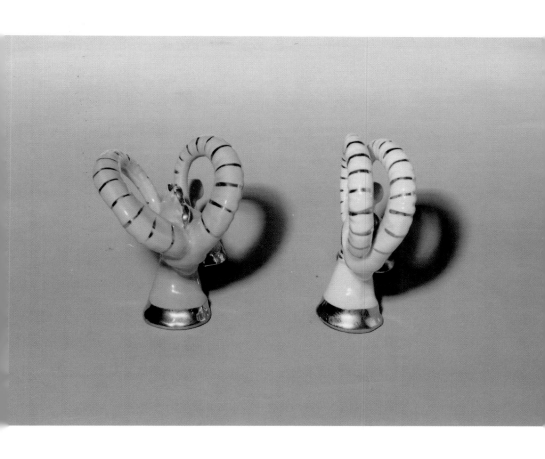

While I have seen several of these rams, I don't believe I have
ever seen two whose horns were at the same angle.

The same ram in pink. Height is 4-1/4 inches. It is unmarked.
Estimated value: $15. *Private Collection.*

This bighorn sheep is 6-7/8 inches high. It is unmarked.
Estimated value: $20. *Carson Collection.*

This skunk looks enough *un*like Grindley that it may not have
been recognized if its paper label had not been present. The
figure is 4 x 4-1/4 inches. Estimated value: $10. *Oravitz
Collection.*

More teal, one of Grindley's most distinctive glazes. The
squirrel stands 3-1/4 inches high, has a paper label on its tail.
Estimated value: $15. *Carson Collection.*

This example is the tallest of the three, 3-1/2 inches. It is unmarked. Estimated value: $15. *Oravitz Collection.*

Unmarked, 3-3/8 inches, and in another distinctive Grindley glaze. Estimated value: $15. *Oravitz Collection.*

Here is something different. The tiger itself, which may have been marketed without the base at some point, is 5 inches high, 8-1/2 inches long. The base is 7/8 of an inch high. The bottom, with its Grindley mark, is shown on page 16. Estimated value: $40. *Oravitz Collection.*

I tried photographing this zebra six ways to Serengeti, but there were just too many stripes to get a good picture. In case you can't decipher this one, the animal has its head turned back over its left shoulder. The zebra is 6 inches high, has a Grindley paper label near its tail. Estimated value: $30. *Carson Collection.*

An unmarked zebra, 5-1/2 inches high. Estimated value: $25. *Oravitz Collection.*

The turtle measures 1-1/2 x 2-3/4 inches. It is unmarked.
Estimated value: $10. *Oravitz Collection.*

A pelican, 3-1/2 inches high. It is not marked. Estimated
value: $10. *Oravitz Collection.*

Zebras? Donkeys? Something else? Whatever they are, their average height is 5-1/8 inches, and none of them is marked. Estimated value: left $15, center $25, right $15. *Oravitz Collection.*

Chapter 6
Salt and Peppers

Here Grindley collectors get a break. Ceramic salt and peppers usually command a premium price because of the many shaker collectors that look for them. For the most part, however, Grindley has failed to light a fire under shaker collectors the way Ceramic Arts Studio, Rosemeade, and even Made-in-Japan shakers have. That translates into having to spend less to acquire them, a circumstance about which few people would complain.

Chicken shakers, 3-3/8 inches high on the left, 3-3/4 inches high on the right. Note that each has a Grindley paper label. Estimated value: $15. *Carson Collection.*

Same birds, different paper label. Heights are the same as the gold ones. Estimated value: $10. *Oravitz Collection.*

Pink with no labels. Heights are 3-1/4 and 3-1/2 inches.
Estimated value: $10. *Carson Collection.*

Inspect this photo carefully and you will find two types of pheasants, those whose tails remain broad at the end and have a slight vee (the pair at left), and those whose tails are more pointed (the pair at right). The pair on the right has a paper label to confirm not only their identity, but also the identity of those in other photos. The pair on the left have not

These penguin shakers are 3-5/8 inches high. The one on the left has a Grindley paper label about halfway up its back. Estimated value: $20. *Oravitz Collection.*

been found with a paper label, and therefore must be considered unconfirmed. However, since all signs point to Grindley, they are being included. That said, the unconfirmed pair at left measures 3-1/4 x 6-1/2 inches. The pair on the right measures 2-3/4 x 6 inches. Estimated value: left not determined, right $10. *Carson Collection.*

This pair, the components of which measure 2-3/4 6-1/8 inches, does have a Grindley paper label. Estimated value: $10. *Carson Collection.*

An unconfirmed pair in gold. Each measures 3-1/2 x 6 inches.
Estimated value: price not determined. *Carson Collection.*

A pink unconfirmed pair, each component being 3-5/8 inches high, 6-1/2 inches long. Estimated value: price not determined. *Oravitz Collection.*

A confirmed but unmarked pair in pink. They measure 3-5/8 x 6-1/4 inches. Estimated value: $10. *Carson Collection.*

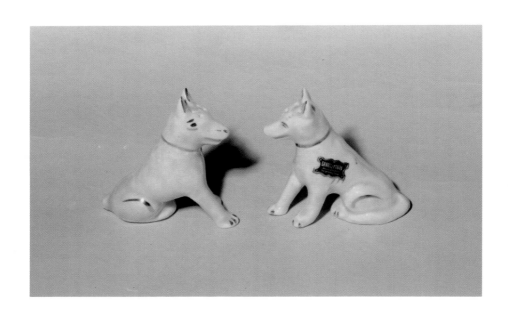

In addition to the Grindley sticker, this pair of dog shakers also has a "Hand painted / Made in USA" paper label that can't be seen in the picture. Each dog is 3 inches high. Estimated value: $10. *Oravitz Collection.*

Height of these marked dog shakers is 2-3/4 inches. Estimated value: $10. *Carson Collection.*

The dogs in gold, 3 inches high and carrying a Grindley paper label. Estimated value: $15. *Oravitz Collection.*

Each of these Scottie shakers stands 3 inches high. One has a
Grindley paper label. Estimated value: $15. *Carson Collection.*

Begging dogs, 2-3/4 inches high, and carrying a Grindley paper label that cannot be seen in the picture. Estimated value: $10. *Carson Collection.*

Monkey shakers, 2-3/4 inches high. They are unmarked.
Estimated value: $10. *Carson Collection.*

Height of these squirrels is 2-7/8 inches high. As you can see,
one has a Grindley paper label. Estimated value: $10. *Carson
Collection.*

Different pair of squirrels, 3-3/8 inches high. Neither of these is marked. Estimated value: $10. *Carson Collection.*

The fish are 2-1/4 inches high. Estimated value: $15. *Oravitz Collection.*

Chapter 7

Miscellaneous Items

Miscellaneous includes the rare figurines of people, a few banks, and pitchers. In addition to what is shown here, known Grindley products include an Elsie cow creamer, and an Elsie breakfast set consisting of a plate, bowl and cup.

Although the glaze color and gold trim of this unmarked pig bank suggests Grindley, it has recently been found with multi-colored decoration and carrying a paper label from the Stanford Pottery, which was also located in Sebring. It is 7-5/8 inches high. Its bottom is shown. Estimated value: $35. *Oravitz Collection.*

Bottom of the pig bank.

The elephant bank is 6-1/2 inches high. This one is not marked but others have been found with Grindley paper labels. Estimated value: $25. *Carson Collection.*

The horse head wall plaque is 5 inches high. Note the Grindley paper label. Rumors persist that a larger one was made, but I have not seen it. One of the same size facing in the opposite direction seems a very likely possibility. Estimated value: $45. *Private Collection*

This Dutch boy cream pitcher stands 4-3/4 inches high. "Grindley" is impressed in its bottom. Estimated value: $20. *Oravitz Collection.*

The lady of this couple is 10 inches high and unmarked. The man is 9-3/4 inches high, has a Grindley paper label. Estimated value: $45 each. *Oravitz Collection.*

Here is the man again, same size and unmarked. Notice that
the feather in his hat is broken. Upon close inspection it is
obvious this was done at the factory prior to decorating,
probably when the piece was removed from the mold. My
guess is that many others, perhaps most, suffered this same
fate considering the placement and the delicate nature of the
feather. Estimated value: $40. *Oravitz Collection.*

Bibliography

Derwich, Jenny B., and Latos, Dr. Mary. *Dictionary Guide to United States Pottery and Porcelain (19th and 20th Century).* Franklin, Michigan: Jenstan, 1984.

Lafferty, James R., Sr., M.A. *The Forties Revisited.* Privately printed, 1968.

Lehner, Lois. *Lehner's Encyclopedia of U.S. Marks on Pottery, Porcelain and Clay.* Paducah, Kentucky: Collector Books, 1988.

Schneider, Mike. *Animal Figures.* West Chester, Pennsylvania: Schiffer Publishing Ltd., 1990.

-----. *Complete Salt and Pepper Shaker Book, The.* Atglen, Pennsylvania: Schiffer Publishing Ltd., 1993.

Index